DEDICATION

This book is dedicated to my family.
To my mother for giving me the courage
to trust and believe in myself.
To my father for teaching me to have a
strong entrepreneurial spirit, drive and determination.
To my brother for always being there when I needed
help, support and understanding.
My family has taught me the importance of
giving and sharing with others.

Debbie Allen

ACKNOWLEDGMENTS

I would like to express my sincere thanks to the many people who helped and encouraged me to complete this book.

Thanks to my dear friends for being such a huge support and and there with me every step of the way.

I would also like to thank my favorite sales and manufacturing associates for giving their input and for sharing with me their "retail stars."

For my knowledge of retail and the learned skill of quality networking, I thank all of my friends through Fashion Alliance in Chicago. Without your willingness to accept me into your prestigious group many years ago, I would not have written this book for so many others in our profession to enjoy and learn by.

And most of all, I want to thank all of the great "retail stars" who shared with us their knowledge, time and success.

Debbie Allen

PREFACE

What an incredible experience it was for me to write this book. I never imagined just how rewarding and educational the experience would be. They say you should write a book when it is burning inside of you. Inside me was a burning desire to read this book, yet it never existed. That is why I decided to create it.

I truly love networking and sharing with other business people. It is a thrill to see someone grow and to succeed in his or her own business. To turn dreams into reality.

As I heard story after story of how each of these retail stars got their start in this industry, I was touched and intrigued by each one of them. It reminded me of my beginnings and of just how far I have come myself. Sometimes we are just too close to it to really see how much we have grown and changed with our businesses.

As you read through these stories and shared thoughts, think about your own growth and the changes that you have made along your journey. And if your journey is just beginning, keep your passion and focus to make your way towards Retail Stardom.

☆☆☆☆

The shared collection of thoughts and ideas in this book are not necessarily my opinion. Each idea and thought will work differently for each retailer. Use what you feel will work best for you.

CONTENTS

Acknowledgments

Preface

Chapter 1
GETTING STARTED
IN THE BUSINESS

There is something special about retail that is different from other industries. Once you become involved, it gets into your blood. It becomes part of you and therefore gives you the passion to continue each day. It is a difficult and demanding business. Retail is ever changing and will always keep you guessing and challenged, trying to figure out the whys and hows of it all. It takes a special individual to survive retail, much less to become a huge success.

There are few in this industry who become true retail stars. These few have many things in common as you will discover in this book. These retailers possess key ingredients that make it work: a true passion for their business and a strong commitment to making it a success. They will do whatever it takes to make it – and not only make it, make it famously. They are open-minded and flexible. Therefore, they never stop learning and growing.

All of these retailers have their own unique stories to tell about how they came upon their demanding, yet rewarding careers in retail. As I heard the stories of how each of these retail stars got their start into this industry, I was motivated and inspired to make my business better in many ways. The experience of these retailers ranges from seven years to over 43 years. The sizes of their locations range from 800 square feet to well over 5,000 square feet; they occupy from one to over 30 locations.

My story . . .

I fell into this business with the help of my mother. Mom wanted to sell her store and move out of state, so she convinced me that it was something I needed to do. I really didn't want anything to do with this business. I didn't know anything about it except that it was fun to go to market – isn't that enough? I couldn't miss out on those buying trips, so I bought the store as a hobby. Some hobby it turned out to be. My first year it was an expensive hobby. Then I quit my other career, and focused on my retail business, got smart and started making some real money. My business background was solid, yet retail was a tough business in which to be successful.

I opened my second store after the first year. From there, I continued to grow and expand beyond my expectations. It was the love of the business and a new challenge that kept me going. Within a six year period, I had grown my business over 10 times. I actually had customers traveling for miles around to shop at my stores, and I couldn't believe what had happened.

After achieving success in my retail stores in the Midwest, I moved on. I sold my two stores and moved to Arizona for a lifestyle change. With retail still in my blood, I opened my third location in Scottsdale. Three years later, I created my professional speaking and consulting firm, *Image Dynamics, Inc.* I have never been satisfied unless I'm growing and changing. That has probably been my greatest asset in business.

☆☆☆☆

"I started out as a stock boy with Ames. From there I went to manager and eventually purchased the store."

Dick has proved that you can have the American Dream. You can make it happen! After 43 years in business and 12 locations, Dick states that his business has never been better, even at a time when many retailers are complaining about the bad economy. Dick's oldest son now runs part of the business while Dick maintains control over the buying and merchandising of the stores. He plans to semi-retire in Sedona, Arizona. With the help of new technology, he can still be in touch with his California stores every day from his Arizona office.

Dick Oliver of Ames; Culver City, CA

☆☆☆☆

From chemical engineer to a retail star in ladies' apparel. Wow, what a switch. I asked Larry just how he made such a transition.

"I was looking for an investment, and I wanted to own a business. Retail was not my passion; it was the last thing I would have thought I would get into. I purchased an existing store because it was a good investment and a great location. The store had a good track record. After purchasing the store, I remodeled it for a new look but kept the name the same.

"I hired a great manager (Susan) with a lot of enthusiasm and experience. I learned a lot about the business from Susan and the previous owner. The previous owner consulted with me and took me to market to learn how to do the buying.

"What I enjoy about this business is making money and seeing my merchandise mix work. There is nothing I enjoy more than a beautiful, well-dressed woman."

Larry Shaw of Private Collections; Las Vegas, NV

Marty's retail experience began when she was working for an upscale boutique. With the knowledge of the industry, Marty was ready to make a change and open her own store. With an excellent customer rapport, Marty already had a great following, and her store was a huge success from day one.

Marty has now experienced 35 years in the industry. Her love for the retail business has helped her remain a success for so many years. Marty regrets that she will be ending her career in retail and retiring soon. She will definitely be missed by her many loyal customers. Marty is a role model in the retail industry – a true Retail Star.

Marty Spencer of Chantilly Place; Riverside, CA

☆☆☆☆

Talk about experience, Sylvia Rosett started in retail when she was just 13 years of age. She began working on the books in her father's business. Her father started out by selling from house to house before he opened his first store 54 years ago. Caplan's has expanded to three families and four locations.

Sylvia Rosett of Caplan's; Chicago, IL

☆☆☆☆

"I worked in a men's store and a shoe store in high school. From there, I started managing Mr. Landon's store and ended up owning the store myself. Mr. Landon was a great mentor. He was also a great friend. He even worked for me for free while I attended school to complete my degree.

"The store started out with only men's clothing and shoes 40 years ago. Ten years ago I added women's apparel. The young men's business changes so fast, you always need to be chasing new lines. The women's division is so different. I am most concerned with controlling markdowns in that department."

Jeff Maloy of Landon's; Ceres, CA

☆☆☆☆

Barbara started out in this industry when she was at a young age of 14, another early bloomer. Retail is in her blood. She loves it so much that she can't get out of the business.

"You must have your heart into it to become successful."

Barbara Strassberger of Prestige; Palo Alto, CA

☆☆☆☆

Georgia started out in retail in a partnership. Within one year she bought out her partner and took off on her own. She now has over 10 years' experience behind her.

"I learned this business from the school of hard knocks. It was difficult to get started, but what I had going for me was good timing back in 1986. If I had to open now, in the 90's, I may not have lasted. I guess I did well from the beginning because I have always been different with my merchandise mix — it's just not the norm. I wanted to make a statement. I did not want to be like everyone else."

Georgia Rosenblat of Iris; Palm Springs, CA

☆☆☆☆

In high school Susan took Latin classes and flunked twice. "My dad wanted me to take Latin, but it was just not for me.

Then I took home economics because it was the only thing available. I enjoyed sewing so much I decided to major in fashion design. That's where I found my love of fashion."

After school Susan worked as an assistant buyer. Later, she moved to Coronado Island and found a store that was for sale.

"I bought the store for the location and changed the name. It was a great opportunity! The past owner was ill and not there very much. It was a good store, but it needed help and new life. I was just the person for the job."

Susan Warmbrodt of The Armoire; Coronado, CA

☆☆☆☆

With her art school background, Stephanie began by painting items on her own wardrobe and tee shirts for friends in her garage. Stephanie's aunt gave her encouragement after hearing all of the compliments she was receiving on her creations.

"When someone came up to me and complimented my outfit, my aunt would say, 'She's a famous designer, and she can paint one for you too.' I started putting outfits together, and the business started to grow. I hired sales associates from Dallas to New York and ran my 5,000 square foot warehouse from California. It was just too hard to run the manufacturing because there is so much to do. I wanted to be more in control of the day to day operation, so I decided to go back into my first love of retail."

Stephanie Meyer of Stephan Cori; Fresno, CA

☆☆☆☆

What a big step up the ladder to success! Ken started out as a stock boy for a women's specialty store and ended up as president and chief executive officer for a chain of nationally acclaimed specialty stores.

"My dad told me to get a job, and having no idea what I wanted in my future career, I ended up in retail. My first break came when the store's buyer needed an assistant. He took me to New York for my first buying trip. When he left the company, I was the only one who knew the job. I eventually went on to becoming president of that company. After the business changed, I moved to Colorado to run a chain of specialty stores. Another opportunity came my way, and I moved again to New York to work directly for a manufacturer. They decided to expand into retail and opened 30 stores across the country."

Kenneth Mizel of Rodier.Paris; Ramsey, NJ

☆☆☆☆

Jennifer has been a buyer of Crystal Cruises for six years. I found this quite interesting when I interviewed Jennifer. She has some additional challenges that the average retailer does not face. I wanted to know how it all worked. How do you get new stock to the ship when it's moving around all over the world? It's not as if your UPS man can just drop deliveries in the back room – of a moving store. It is a big challenge to have those deliveries sent to the ship or even to plan. At any time, weather problems or even international disasters might occur.

"I earned my stripes in the department stores while I was in the buying offices and in store management for over 16 years. I worked in many different departments. That helped me learn to be a good buyer for the four stores aboard each ship. It's a different type of retail when you are buying for a ship. Working in so many different departments helped me learn the difference. I buy everything from aspirin to better sportswear now.

"At age 35, I short circuited and quit the department store to work on a cruise ship. I helped set up retail stores on a new ship. Along with this, I started my own jewelry and accessory business called Razzle Dazzle. I was busy with 200 store accounts of my own and worked on the ship when I could take off for a few weeks at a time. My glory with Razzle Dazzle is that I invented a key item in the industry – the tee shirt ring."

Jennifer Chadney of Crystal Cruises; Los Angeles, CA

☆☆☆☆

Loree started out with a very small retail space, only 150 square feet. Since the store was so tiny, she named it the Clothes Crack. She only had enough room to sell tops at that time. As the business grew, she felt comfortable with a move and store expansion.

"I had to change the name since the store was no longer a tiny space. I named it G. Nonni after my grandmother who had recently passed away. My grandmother had been in retail all of her life – she was my inspiration! The G stands for grandmother, and Nonni is what she was called by the family.

"I was fortunate to have good experience from working in department stores as a buyer and from the knowledge of my husband's wholesale clothing business. Having a good eye also helped to know what to look for in fashion. My college education in fashion design was useful for fabric selection. Along with one and one half years of fashion design, I had a degree in sociology. This was probably the most important aspect of my education, to know how to work with people."

With all of Loree's knowledge and determination, she has remained successful in this industry for 21 years. That's an incredible feat in this ever-changing business.

Loree Scarborough of G. Nonni; Long Beach, CA

☆☆☆☆

The original store opened in the early 50's, when Bill's parents started out. Bill graduated from college and then joined his parents in the business. They opened multiple locations to take care of the family. Pat joined the business shortly after having children. Pat learned the business from on-the-job training, relying on the experience of the original owners and asking questions in the market. She listened to other store owners to see what ideas could be applied to their businesses.

Bill and Pat Kassul of Personality Shoppe; Rochelle, IL

☆☆☆☆

"I would never have opened a store if I hadn't been fired from my job. I probably would have just continued working for someone else. Losing my job gave me the incentive to open up for myself. The best thing I had going for me when I opened was my name; I was known across the country from my previous job. That's why I named the store after myself."

Helen Lyall of Helen Lyall; Vallejo, CA

☆☆☆☆

Laura grew up in the people business. She started working in the family's restaurant when she was 12 years old. From there, she learned good work ethics and how to work well with people. Laura took fashion merchandising, then started

17

to work in a Dallas apparel center showroom, learning the wholesale end of the business. With her experiences helping her along the way, she opened her first store seven years ago.

Laura Garduno of Gee Lorretta; Albuquerque, NM

☆☆☆☆

"I started out with a 400 square foot store to test out the business. At the beginning I sold only accessory items and my display pieces that I had purchased from an interior design store.

"I found out quickly that I had to move from this bad location. An opportunity came to me one day when the manager of a local resort came into my store and loved it. I moved to that resort location and found that the business was much different there. I was scared to death. I had wanted a small space, and 1,500 square feet was all that was available. That seemed so big to me, how would I fill it up with accessories and a few clothing items? I found out that when I started purchasing clothing it was easy to fill up the space. I was so glad that I took the risk and moved to this new location. It made all the difference in the world."

Susan Liss of Compliments; La Quinta, CA

☆☆☆☆

"I heard this voice from above one day — it was so loud, it actually made me jump '. . . *I am training you to do this work. Go home and start a garage sale. Go ahead and do it today!'*

"I didn't want to learn this business. I wanted to stay home and raise my six children. Why is this voice telling me this? I didn't know why, but I went home and started on my first garage sale. Shortly after this, I was thrown a major curve in my life. My husband lost his store, and we divorced. I was then forced to make it on my own. I had very little to live on when I got started. I sold my furniture and children's toys — whatever I needed to, to make ends meet and raise my family. My garage sales got bigger and bigger, and I managed to make enough money to start my retail business."

Mona started her own store by purchasing a home with a garage in a small town of Indiana. The garage had been converted into a hat shop in this residential area. The hat shop had existed there for 50 years. After purchasing the home, Mona fought with the city for six months for rezoning to carry apparel in the shop. The store started with 1,100 square feet and has been expanded to 3,000 square feet 13 years later. Her newest addition was an outside tent which was up for six months of the year. It has now been added as the Great Room. "I was selling stock from my basement. I did not have the room to put it all out.

"I started with a $10,000 investment into my business. I have proved you can start small. You don't need a lot of money to make it work — just the fortitude to work 70 hours a week and do whatever it takes to make it happen. You need a vision! If you have something to fall back on, you won't work as hard. I didn't have anything to fall back on — I had to survive for my family."

Mona Cramer of Little House; LaPorte, IN

☆☆☆☆

A dynamic mother and daughter teamed up to make a huge success of retail. With the daughter's good taste in fashion and the mother's expertise in business, it was a natural.

"The key to a great store is the location, so we wanted to

make that work for us. We found a store that had previously been a children's book store. The location was great — right on Main Street. Yet the building was old, and the landlord would not help us out with repairs. It had no heat, no air conditioning, and no hot water, and it was filthy dirty. We had to remodel it and put it together in about 30 days. We had so much to do to make it work, but it ended up turning out darling. We couldn't believe it was the same store."

Deanne Westen of Panache; San Jose, CA

☆☆☆☆

"I was looking for a change in my life after a divorce. So when I was asked to work in a small gift shop, I thought it would be fun. After working there for a while, I started purchasing clothing to carry in the corner of the store. It started transforming into more and more. Next thing I knew, I was buying the store. I was joined by my daughter Starr. Starr is such an integral part of the business. Together we make a great team."

Carolyn Walker of Flair Boutique; Stockton, CA

☆☆☆☆

"I was a hairstylist and started buying for the boutique area of my salon. I traveled to Europe and brought back clothing to sell. I started to build a strong customer base. As the sales grew, I needed more room to store the inventory. The boutique area of the salon was quite small, so we could only display one size of an item. I rented an apartment near the store for additional stock and eventually moved to a 3,000 foot location. I now sell everything from sportswear to dressy apparel. My success came from the good customer base I had established in the salon."

Manije Windell of Manije' Boutique; Burlingame, CA

☆☆☆☆

Pam started her 23-year-old company as a one person gift and accessory shop by using money she saved working as a school teacher by day and a waitress by night. "I gave up the security of being a tenured teacher because I was committed to making retail work." Pam has learned to think big through her creative mind and brainstorming techniques.

Today, Pam owns and operates 18 specialty shops located in airports and five-star resorts in Arizona and California. Her company employs 150 people, 67% of whom are minorities. The Delstar Group now grosses more in one day than it did its entire first year in business. Pam has won numerous awards, including Best of America, the Blue Chip Award, Retail Entrepreneur of the Year Award for 1989 and National Socially Responsible Entrepreneur for 1992.

As I entered the Delstar corporate offices, I felt as if I were in a wonderful fantasy land with the incredible celestial and angel decor. It is like no other corporate office I've seen. Pam gave me a tour of the headquarters, which includes a training room, interview room and several offices for other departments. On the walls were photos of their numerous retail locations and other Delstar memorabilia. The office even has a full cafe with a commercial popcorn machine. "We serve popcorn every day for our staff. It's just one way of having a good time around the office."

Pam Del Duca of Delstar Group; Phoenix, AZ

☆☆☆☆

Audrey's parents were in retail for many years. They started out with Hawaiian curio shops and later added Hawaiian sportswear. Her dad asked Audrey one day if she wanted to open a shop. "It was an incredible location. It looked like an Italian villa — that's where the name Villa Roma came from.

"As my customer base grew, the store became very successful. We had nine dressing rooms full with 10 more people waiting in line. I attribute my sister's knowledge for this success. She was working for *Seventeen* magazine, a hot publication in the late 60's. I started paying attention to this magazine and carried the clothing found in the publication. At that time, the strong trends were hot pants and mini skirts. Fashion took a strong turn at that time for the masses. Boutiques were the hot new thing. It was an exciting time.

"I hosted fashion shows in high schools to create this strong new customer base. As our customers grew up, we changed along with them. We added a second store at that time. I wanted my second store to have a very unusual name that people would remember. What could be more decadent than Chocolates for Breakfast? I named my store that because I wanted the customer to know that it was the best of taste, superior service and exquisite clothing.

"We were the #1 grossing store in the entire area for a very long time. After new high-end stores came in, it started to cut into our business, so we changed our mix of merchandise again."

Audrey Fu of Villa Roma & Chocolates for Breakfast; Honolulu, HI

Chapter 2
SURVIVAL
AND SUCCESS

To survive in the retail industry is a success in itself. All of the retailers in this book have had their difficult times in business. The difference between them and so many others is that they learned from their mistakes and continued in a new direction towards success. They have learned that mistakes are just "Big Lessons." They have learned to listen to those lessons and to believe in themselves and their businesses.

☆☆☆☆

My survival . . .

I learned that my customer base was very different in a resort community. My customers told me quickly what type of merchandise would work. I did a lot of markdowns at first. I thought I knew a lot about retail when I opened my third store, yet I found out I had to learn it all over again. It is much more difficult to make it in a resort community. The merchandise mix is much different, the competition is stiff, and the rent and expenses are triple what I was paying in a small town. I learned to adjust quickly. I got rid of merchandise that was not selling and tried new lines.

23

I am always determined to make it work, looking for new opportunities to make my business grow. I keep my creativity working for me by staying fresh and new. I concentrated on getting known in my new community as an expert in my field by joining many local organizations and by quality networking. I have been featured on magazine covers, in newspaper articles and on radio talk shows in the Phoenix area through networking opportunities and speaking engagements. This has built a strong recognition for my business.

✩✩✩✩

Have you considered writing a complete "mission statement" for your business? First, you have to understand just what this "mission statement" is all about. This should be your written declaration of your expectations from your business. It is what others will come to know you by. What is your purpose and principal undertaking as a business owner? Take some time to really think about this. One store owner I interviewed had very specific ideas and objectives down in writing for her business. If you want to create it – you must write it down!

Mission Statement . . .

"To create an environment in which we can help our customers look and feel better about themselves. This can be obtained by striving to keep an honest and open communication with our clients, therefore learning and anticipating their wants and needs. We are committed to being available to them and doing everything we can to make their shopping experience rewarding, fun and fulfilling."

Loree Scarborough of G. Nonni; Long Beach, CA

✩✩✩✩

When Jeff's store burned down, he had to make a decision fast. Should he rebuild at the same location or move the store? He made the decision to move to a new location and did so within 30 days. Jeff turned a disaster into a great opportunity with his decision to move to an even better location. He proved that even through devastation you can make the best of your business.

Knowing how to bounce back and land on top is what has made Jeff such a huge success. During hard times he reduced his overhead and downsized his staff to keep his business profitable.

Jeff Maloy of Landon's; Ceres, CA

☆☆☆☆

"Two years ago, the company went through major restructuring in France and changed the direction of the merchandise. The company ran into problems because they were getting stale. The merchandise looked matronly with no image or direction. We changed that for the better and now are back into making a fashion statement. We are the store for the woman of the 90's. Dollar for dollar, I feel we make the best clothes in the world.

"The French have worked very hard to understand this business in the U.S. They are now planning a major expansion program by adding 10 stores within the year."

Kenneth Mizel of Rodier.Paris; Ramsey, NJ

☆☆☆☆

"We are a five star plus rated ship. The ships cater to an affluent guest and travel around the world. The cruise business is like no other business. Our merchandise is purchased for itineraries rather than seasons and oftentimes has to be shipped all over the world in order to reach the ships. Yes . . . we have a captive audience. However, we must provide them with new and different things to attract their attention. They have all been shopping prior to getting on board. Their suitcases are full of new cruise wear already. We have approximately a 40% return rate of guests, which means that we must constantly have new merchandise, new logo programs, etc.

"Being flexible and able to identify potential problems is always helpful when faced with surprise problems. Crystal Cruises has weathered the recent hard business times with good business, primarily due to the fact that we have been open in our thinking and realize that the world of customers has gone promotional. Even though we didn't want to merchandise in a promotional world, we know that it is important to doing business these days. In order to weather those storms, we have developed more and more promotions, whether it be a sale incentive, gift with purchase or a one day sale. We have learned to capture business during the recent hard times."

Jennifer Chadney of Crystal Cruises; Los Angeles, CA

☆☆☆☆

A personal challenge . . . "I will do whatever it takes to make it work. I have always had wonderful mentors in my life. I always look at what has made it work for them. One of my mentors is in a wheelchair – she has such perserverance and is such an incredible woman.

"I talk to people all the time – I'm always networking. When something is not working for me, I look at others to see what they are doing and just how I can turn it around to work for me. I am open minded and have learned to be a good listener."

Stephanie Meyer of Stephan Cori; Fresno, CA

☆☆☆☆

"I was an instant success with the experience I had from the bottom up. I didn't know what I couldn't do. I never set limits on myself.

"I had a role model that kept me going. The number one retailer in my mind is Stanley Marcus, the founder of Neiman Marcus.

"We learned what our specialization was early on. We have learned to keep changing it just slightly by fine tuning our buying."

Dick Oliver of Ames; Culver City, CA

☆☆☆☆

"Staying focused all the time is my major factor. Not every day is great, but you must stay positive and ready to go to work the next day.

"I put all my blood, sweat and tears into it. And yes, there were tears! I learned to stick with it and be flexible. My husband has been a great support system."

Susan Warmbrodt of The Armoire; Coronado, CA

☆☆☆☆

"We started out with a niche and never changed it. A sure death in this business is when you try to be all things to all people."

Kent Hamrick of Eric Kent; Evanston, IL

☆☆☆☆

"It was difficult when Las Vegas lost a large part of the trade from Mexico. It was a big part of our business.

"My survival tool is a good business and financial background. Making budgets comes natural for me. I work on keeping a close eye and control on my cost of doing business."

Larry Shay of Private Collections; Las Vegas; NV

☆☆☆☆

"It doesn't matter how many years you are in business, you must continually make changes. Pay attention to what customers are buying and change your merchandise somewhat.

"Other stores in the same mall location are always complaining that business is bad. They say it's the mall, the weather, the city, etc. If there is a problem in my store, I need to look in the mirror and say maybe I'm doing something wrong. Maybe I'm the reason business is not as good as it should be. So I think, ' what can I do to make it better?' When my store was growing so quickly, I thought I could do no wrong. Sometimes it catches up to you."

Even though business figures have dropped, Mary has kept the same profit margin. Remember, it's all in your bottom line. That's what really counts! Sometimes, with less volume or even by downsizing your store, your profits can be higher.

Don't get too hung up on making high numbers if it's not working out the best for you.

Mary Black of Hilda; Park City, UT

☆☆☆☆

"We had to close our campus store when the 70's changed fashion. We could not make the same profit by selling tie dyed tee shirts and bell bottom jeans.

"One of our stores had been in the same downtown location for 15 years. We had to close that store because the building was so old and run down. The landlord would not do repairs that were necessary. After closing the store, we expanded our original store which was doing extremely well.

"Our Rochelle store continues to do well because we are always changing along with the market and paying attention to what is selling. We build on categories in the store. We had gold jewelry, furs and high-end dresses when they were really hot fashion statements. We always try to stay on top of the item of the season and make our selection to reflect the specialty store look."

Bill and Pat Kassul of Personality Shoppe; Rochelle, IL

☆☆☆☆

"We have survived so many years because of our personal attention. I still have my own personal accounts that I work with. I call up my customer and tell her what I have for her, and she comes in. You have to show the customers you have interest in them."

Sylvia Rosett of Caplan's; Chicago, IL

"I have always been flexible and changed with the times. I have learned how to change midstream and go in another direction. You can't let your ego get in the way. A lot of store owners will hang onto the merchandise in their stores, even when it is not selling. You need to get rid of your mistakes. Everyone makes them — take the loss and move on."

Sue Gantz of My Sister's Circus; Chicago, IL

☆☆☆☆

"In my first year in retail, I had no clue about marketing. I was so naive — I selected a space in a courtyard hidden from the public. I was paying too much rent, and I had signed an iron-clad five-year lease. I wanted to move because I knew I had selected a bad location, so I kept looking for a better location and was determined to survive those first five years. There were stores around me that went out of business within six months. It was a very difficult time in Arizona with the 100-year flood, the gas shortage and the recession. Tourism was down drastically during those three years.

"When I finally moved to a better location, my business took off. I started with 800 square feet, went to 2,000 and then to 4,000 square feet. From there, I bought the building.

"A big break came when I heard about retail opportunities at the airport in a new terminal. I wrote to the airport for two years to make sure I was sent a bid packet. The rents are extremely high and the process can be very political, but I knew the airport had great potential. It takes a combination of a great location, the right merchandise at the right price, a visually exciting store and excellent customer service to survive in an airport. The main reason our stores have survived is that we pay attention to every detail. If it has my name on it, I want it to be great!

"No matter how big we are, we still run our company like a small business. We treat people as we would like to be treated. We believe in the community and contribute to organizations, and we recruit disadvantaged people and give them a chance at a better livelihood. We help them break barriers by teaching them business skills as well as life skills that give them more self-respect and self-esteem."

Pam has such a passion for helping others. She believes what goes around comes around. She told me of a story in which they gave a homeless woman a job and trained her in retail. This woman ended up being a top salesperson for the company.

Pam Del Duca of Delstar Group; Phoenix, AZ

✩✩✩✩

"The key to our growth and success is our great locations in the top Hawaiian resorts. The resorts have a lot of foot traffic – we sell because of the volume of customers."

Larry Langley of Casual Aire; Honolulu, HI

✩✩✩✩

"My survival comes from keeping on top of everything daily. I focus on my clients' wishes and needs. You must do this to survive and become successful. Personal service is everything!"

Carolyn Walker of Flair Boutique; Stockton, CA

✩✩✩✩

"I believe in thinking and staying positive. Your business is only as good as the hard work you put into it. I have been in my store and involved all the time to make it work. I don't know of any way of making it other than working hard."

Margo Miller of Margo's; Newhall, CA

☆☆☆☆

"My art background has really helped me, even though I was lacking in business skills. I have a good sense of color. I can put creative combinations of color together and unique displays and make it all work. My competitor had no idea what my ability was when I moved to this new location, but as soon as she saw my first window display, she couldn't believe what I had done."

Susan Liss of Compliments; La Quinta, CA

☆☆☆☆

"I opened a store in a mall location and found that the business was very difficult for my type of clientele. I built my own business on a very busy commercial street. I spared no expense to make it the best looking store in town. I spent a lot of money on the decor, but I believe that it has paid off. My holiday business was up 100% from my previous store the first year. Overall, my yearly increase was up 55%. I took a chance and it was very successful."

Laura Garduno of Gee Lorretta; Albuquerque, NM

☆☆☆☆

"I should have worked with someone on my open-to-buy to start out. We did not have enough inventory. But we did buy the right lines because we sold almost everything we had the first week we opened. What we did have was different and great. No one helped us buy at market. Luckily, we had a good eye for fashion.

"Everything was going great the first couple of months we were in business. It seemed as if we could do no wrong. Then the earthquake came. It damaged the street in front of our store. Since the damage was already there, the city decided to do a complete streetscape. My customers had to park far from the store and walk to us. It really affected our business. More problems continued with the war and the California fires. It was difficult to get through those hard times, but we hung in there and survived.

"We survived because we had a positive attitude. We are always friendly to our customers. On top of that, we continually look for new lines and move the store around to make it look fresh. We color coordinate the store from earth tones to different shades. This makes it easy on the eye and easier to shop."

Deanne Westen of Panache; San Jose, CA

☆☆☆☆

"I started by purchasing off-price merchandise from factories until I could build up my credit. I traveled to factories in the middle of the night. I left at midnight, traveled to the location, picked up the merchandise and was back home the next day to work.

"I have very low overhead since I own the home where my store is located. I only pay the taxes, but no rent. My build-out was inexpensive since the shop already existed. I just painted the store. It's not fancy – just basic, with lots of inventory.

"I starved for three years just trying to keep my store alive, continuing with my garage sale business to help out on the side. I reinvested all my profits back into the business by purchasing more inventory. I took very little out of the business as it was growing. I just kept putting it back in. My business volume really peaked after six years.

"Overbuying really hurt me. I have now learned to adjust my inventory, and my business is more profitable than ever. I am always trying to learn how to make it better."

What an incredible lady. I really admire Mona for all of her hard work and strong determination. Her store is like no other store I have ever seen – what a great operation!

Mona Cramer of Little House; LaPorte, IN

☆☆☆☆

"I have always changed with the times. You have to change to survive. We had to bring in items that people could afford because the times had changed. We changed our pricing and the store prospered again.

"The most devastating thing that happened to us was three years ago. We lost our lease for Villa Roma after 26 years. Another large chain store was coming in and needed our space. I fought to keep our space, but in the end we moved our location to another shopping mall. The new landlord was wonderful. He did everything to make it work for us. We didn't do as much volume as the other location, but we made adjustments that worked for us. We cut our overhead and reduced staff. Our rent was lower at this new location, so our profit was still good. We also had to drastically change our mix again. We sold young sexy fashions at the first location, and we now have a completely different customer base, the working girl."

Audrey Fu of Villa Roma & Chocolates for Breakfast; Honolulu, HI

"We had no experience when we started in this business. We had no idea all of the problems that would arise. The freeway ramp was closed for six months, diverting the traffic pattern away from our store. The recession hit us hard too, but we did survive. The key to our survival was that we were up front and honest with our vendors from the very beginning. We took the time to explain to them what was going on, and they helped us through it. Because of that open communication with these vendors, we are still here today. We have continued to stay loyal to these same vendors and are doing great business with them."

Russ & Becky Casenhiser of La Galleria; Tustin, CA

☆☆☆☆

Bruce handles customer service relations and teaches customer service skills to the sales staff and managers of Ames. Bruce is a great teacher who believes in creating a staff that thinks on its own.

"My job is to work myself out of a job because the employees have learned how to be good problem solvers. The entire operation is more powerful if everyone is growing and sharing ideas. This always solves more problems. I teach the staff to use what they already know. I just bring it out in them.

"When I came into this business, one of the first things I said was that I have been a customer all my life, and my needs aren't being met. I needed to turn that around."

Bruce came into the company with no retail experience, yet he was a key player in turning the stores around and making them grow. His job is to coach, consult and motivate the staff.

Bruce Hird of Ames; Culver City, CA   35

Chapter 3
BEYOND EXPECTATION CUSTOMER SERVICE

Show that you appreciate your customers all the time by creating friendships. Always give your customers more than they expect. Promise less and give more! Your customers have been burned before, so they are just waiting for you to make a mistake. Be consistent with your service, and always come through on your promises.

Go beyond their expectation every day, and they will run back to your store time and time again to do business with you. I have always had great service in my store, but when I started to make it a priority to be consistent and to go beyond what we had promised, I saw a drastic change and growth in my business. Believe me, it works.

One of the things I do in my business to go beyond customers' expectations is to send them a $20 welcome gift certificate. These certificates are mailed out the day after the customer signs up on the mailing list along with a special, hand written note. We also send out $20 certificates with birthday cards. We keep two files for our special orders to make sure the customer is followed up. My manager, who is also my mother, Nancy Roath, calls in the special orders and works on keeping on top of these all the time. It is so important to follow through and keep in contact with the customer. If we make a mistake or something is not delivered as we promised, we give our customer a nice gift or free alterations to make up for it.

☆☆☆☆

"Customer service is extremely important. Everyone wants to feel important. This must be conveyed to your employees. Your staff needs to send thank you letters and make phone calls to inform your customers of sales, events and new merchandise. Your employees should call your customers by name. People love to hear their names!"

Jennifer Chadney of Crystal Cruises; Los Angeles, CA

☆☆☆☆

"To learn how we are doing with customer service, we use a secret shopper service in our stores. I don't think we are as good as we could be. We are about 75% of where I would like to see us in customer service. To improve in this area, we need to see a more structured training program for our staff, and we plan to do that. We also need to recognize our problems more quickly."

Kenneth Mizel of Rodier.Paris; Ramsey, NJ

☆☆☆☆

"I send out birthday gift certificates ranging from $25 to $100, depending on the customer. I offer more for that customer who has continued to be loyal and supportive over the years.

"I do very few store promotions because my customer base is always changing from week to week. A promotion does not bring customers into my store because most of my business is from tourists. They come in because of my unique lines of clothing. I make sure that when they come into my store, I am personally available for the clients. Service is our specialty. There is nothing we will not do for our customers."

Georgia Rosenblat of Iris; Palm Springs, CA

☆☆☆☆

"We pay close attention to our merchandise mix and what our customer really wants. I went to market and picked out all of the clothing for an entire wedding, from the bride to the guests. They loved everything I picked out because I really try to get to know what my customers want."

Barbara Strassberger of Prestige; Palo Alto, CA

☆☆☆☆

"I am flexible with my policies and will take returns. I talk to my customers and find out what I can do to make them happy. Sometimes the customers have it built up in their minds that they are going to have to fight with you on a return. I just listen to them and find out a way to turn it around."

Mary Black of Hilda; Park City, UT

☆☆☆☆

"When customers are in the store, they are the main priority. My only concern is to take care of them. We don't have a lot of foot traffic, so we really have to work with customers when they come in. We have a very limited customer base since we are in a small town."

Pat Kassul of Personality Shoppe; Rochelle, IL

"We do a lot of little things for our customers that add up to one big thing – great customer service. We take the time to get to know our customers. By knowing our customers' purchase history, we can service them better. Our computer is set up to let us know what a customer has purchased in the past. My sales staff can work with that information to help the customer coordinate new items with other items in her wardrobe. Our special orders are also set up on a computer program that we created. The program will let us know when an item was promised to a customer so we can keep up on this at all times. We could not do this manually because we have from 75 to 200 items on special order at one time."

Russ & Becky Casenhiser of La Galleria; Tustin, CA

✩✩✩✩

Making a call to a customer to come into her store to check out new merchandise is not enough for one star retailer. Marty goes one better by setting up the dressing room before her customer arrives. She then orders lunch for her customer from the restaurant next door. Wow, now that's beyond expectation customer service!

Marty treats her V.I.P. customers by sending them flowers on special occasions. In addition, she sends birthday and anniversary cards, offering special store discounts.

Marty Spencer of Chantilly Place; Riverside, CA

✩✩✩✩

When discount stores opened around Kathleen's business, she had to learn to compete with "real" competition.

"My clientele trusts me, and they bring their friends and relatives to my store. I take better care of my customers than my competition, and that keeps them coming back for more. I take care of them better because I know them personally and will bend over backwards to help them.

"If a customer needs an outfit fast, we can turn around and complete an alteration in two hours. I love it when my customers come to me and tell me that my service and staff are so much nicer than the other stores around me."

Kathleen Gubler of Evelyn's; St. George, UT

☆☆☆☆

"Our pricing is competitive. Personalized service is important to us. We can have alterations back in one day, and we deliver to their hotel rooms.

"We work hard on our special orders by following up all the time. We take the time to call the companies, make sure the item is available and find out when it can be shipped. We talk to our suppliers every day."

Larry Shay of Private Collections; Las Vegas, NV.

☆☆☆☆

"We spend a lot of time on presentation and merchandising – our newest store is incredible!

"You need to be specialized in this business. It is like a three-legged stool. One leg is buying and merchandising, the second is administration, and the third leg is the presentation. If you kick out one leg, the stool falls."

Dick Oliver of Ames; Culver City, CA

"I set one big goal a year and really work on that goal. It works better for me if I can get totally focused on one thing at a time. My goal this year is to create better customer loyalty. I ask myself, 'what can we do to make our customers think about us all the time?'"

Mona Cramer of Little House; LaPorte, IN

☆☆☆☆

"I do personal shopping as a service for my customers. I will charge them a small flat fee of $100 per day, and I will shop with them for everything from underwear to shoes. I really enjoy doing that, and I get a lot of thank you cards from my customers because of this special service."

Deanne Westen of Panache; San Jose, CA

☆☆☆☆

"We have a $1,000 club. When customers purchase $1,000 of regular priced merchandise, they receive a $100 gift certificate to use on their next purchase. They must complete the total purchase within one year. Our computer keeps track of the purchases and will automatically print a gift certificate when a customer reaches $1,000. The computer will also print out notices to the customers if they are getting close to the year's end. The notice tells the customers how much they need to spend to receive the $100 gift certificate.

"Customers will buy in my store more often because of this club offer. If they see a line or group in another store, they will call us to see if we carry the merchandise. They want to buy it from us so that they get the credit on their club card."

Laura Garduno of Gee Lorretta; Albuquerque, NM

"I have a very personalized business. I give my customers a lot of attention. I am on my sales floor all day long, sometimes working a 12 hour day. I never get tired of working on the floor with my customers even after 19 years of owning my store. I want to pamper my customers all the time. I will even make evening appointments if it is convenient for my customers. My store hours don't matter – I need to be available to them.

"During the holidays, I give my top 40 customers very nice gifts. I want to acknowledge my customers all the time. When I'm out for dinner and see one of my good customers, I will order a bottle of wine and send it over to his or her table."

Helen Lyall of Helen Lyall; Vallejo, CA

☆☆☆☆

"The best thing we do for our customers is to have long hours. We are open 365 days a year. Yes, even Christmas because it is always busy here. We are open from 8:00 a.m. to 10:00 p.m. every day. When people are on vacation, they want us to be open – so we are."

Larry Langley of Casual Aire; Honolulu, HI

☆☆☆☆

"I had a customer who needed a pair of shoes for the evening, and with no shoe stores in the area, I took off my shoes and offered them to her to wear. That gave me the idea to sell shoes in my store. It is now a big part of my business.

"My store's packaging is great. Every bag that leaves the store has tons of curly ribbon tied on it. This very dressy gift wrapping adds that special touch. There is no charge to my customers for this service, and it comes back to me when other people notice the packaging and know what store it came from. With a nice purchase, I give my customers gifts also."

Susan Liss of Compliments; La Quinta, CA

☆☆☆☆

I was so impressed with this lady. I could tell that she is great with her customers by the numerous times she called me by my name during our interview. Margo knows how to listen and how to make people feel special. She loves working with her customers on the floor, even after 21 years in the retail business.

"I carry everything from head to toe for the total look. My inventory includes shoes, hosiery, lingerie and apparel for career, casual and evening wear, and, of course, a complete accessory line to finish the look from casual to dressy. We recently started carrying gifts items as well, and they are selling very well. It takes a lot more work buying, but it's worth the effort. I want to give my customer the complete look.

"I am very flexible with my policies. Whatever it takes to make my customers happy is what I want to achieve. When the owner is on the premises, it is hard not to bend the rules. If I'm not there, the staff can always fall back on the store policies as their guidelines."

Margo Miller of Margo's; Newhall, CA

☆☆☆☆

"I record my customers' requests in a customer base file that we do all by hand. We make a lot of phone calls and send lots of handwritten notes when new lines arrive."

Manije Windell of Manije' Boutique; Burlingame, CA

☆☆☆☆

"My job doesn't stop when I leave the store. I go home and bake homemade cookies almost every night to serve to my customers with fresh roasted coffee.

"I add a special touch with my beautiful gift wrap. I will add flowers and extra ribbon to the package, depending on the price of the item. It's a great service that my customers love."

Carolyn Walker of Flair Boutique; Stockton, CA

☆☆☆☆

"I have the most dedicated and knowledgeable staff. Most of them have been with me for 10 to 15 years. My employees love fashion – they live and breathe it every day. They will go out of their way for a customer – even pick up a customer's dry cleaning on their time off. They will deliver the customers' purchases, take them shoe shopping in the mall and share tips on hairstyling. Each of my salespeople have their own customer list, and they know their customers by name."

Audrey Fu of Villa Roma & Chocolates for Breakfast; Honolulu, HI

Chapter 4
THE S.T.A.F.F.
SALES • TEAMS • ATTRIBUTE
FAMOUS • FORMULA

I offer a group commission that is based on a monthly quota for the store. If the quota is not achieved that month, they don't receive that bonus. My staff gets involved in the day to day business because they have a goal to work toward. I have added bonuses on personal sales that we call "tips" in addition to their hourly wage and quota bonus. This is a real motivator for my staff. The bonus is based mostly on a group commission, and that is why they work so well as a team. Everyone helps one another with sales because they are all working for the same goal.

I want my staff to think for themselves – to be self-motivated. I delegate the area that supports their strengths. Everyone has jobs that they are responsible for in the areas that they do their best work. They are all great, and they can run the store well without me there all the time. Since I travel so much and have my other career with Image Dynamics, I very seldom can work on my sales floor. I need their input all the time to let me know what is happening in the business, to keep me on top of things.

As my business grew, my job changed. It will continue to change in the future. That is why it is so important to have a structured program in place so that my staff knows what is expected of them. My job now is to oversee the business, work on all promotions and advertising and do all of the buying for the store. I have to count on my staff to run the day to day business. I just keep them motivated.

Along with regular monthly meetings, I plan a full day meeting at least twice a year called "Success Through Collective Energy." During this full day meeting we build strategies and set goals and promotions for the upcoming season. At this time, I will bring in a facilitator to keep our meeting on track. We not only share and learn from one another, we get more connected as a team. It is amazing how much we can accomplish in this day. I make sure that the day is special for them by having the meeting at a beautiful club and adding a fabulous lunch and some fun time. I try to let my employees know how much they are appreciated.

Thank you to my incredible team – you make my business successful because you care!

☆☆☆☆

Barbara keeps her staff motivated with her own enthusiasm and self-motivation. She does everything from vacuuming and cleaning to making personalized telephone calls to her customers.

"Because I do it all, everyone else works as a team. How can you ask someone to do something that you won't do yourself? I work fast and like to accomplish a lot in a day. I have learned that everyone is different and not everyone works the same way. Over time, I have learned to respect that."

Barbara Strassberger of Prestige; Palo Alto, CA

"I always plan in-store meetings. We work together as a team. When new merchandise arrives, we try it on and compare notes."

Georgia does not offer an individual commission on sales, except for spiffs (bonuses) on multiple sales.

"I don't want my customer attacked when she walks into my store. I resent it when I go into a store and salespeople do that to me. So I know my customer will resent it too. I want my customer to feel at home and at ease in my store."

Example of spiffs (bonus) on multiple sales:

The first sale is for the house. The second item on the same receipt is worth a $2 spiff. The third item on the same receipt is worth a $3 spiff. The fourth item on the same receipt is worth an additional $5 spiff. (On a sale of four items, the sales staff can make up to $10 per receipt.) Add on sales must be a minimum value amount required by the store. Bonuses are paid on all sales at the end of each week.

Georgia Rosenblat of Iris; Palm Springs, CA

☆☆☆☆

"Most of my staff has been with the store for a number of years. We have the same tourists coming back to the store, and they like to see the same staff.

"Susan, my manager, has a lot of experience. She motivates the staff because she projects her dynamics on the floor. Susan gets everyone excited, and they sell more. We have great merchandise to sell, and we get our staff thrilled about all the new merchandise as it arrives. They are selling enthusiasm and emotion to our customers."

Larry Shay of Private Collections; Las Vegas, NV

☆☆☆☆

"It is the people that make the store. That is the name of the game. When I came on board at this company, I had to re-place about 75% of the staff. In 1994 we had to rebuild our stores, and we now find a more motivated staff. We are really starting to see the results from this change now."

Kenneth Mizel of Rodier.Paris; Ramsey, NJ

☆☆☆☆

"We rely heavily on our on-board managers to motivate the staff, as the ship is often 6,000 miles away from us. However, I do develop contests and spiffs to help motivate the team. The staff is also involved in setting up these con-tests. They take more ownership of the contest if they par-ticipate in the planning, thus making the event more suc-cessful.

"Positive recognition is key to the success of any business. I constantly recognize sales performance and good ideas de-veloped by the staff.

"The staff has learned to be self-motivating because they are so involved in the business. Each day the staff presents a merchandise meeting to discuss merchandise benefits and new sales techniques."

Jennifer Chadney of Crystal Cruises; Los Angeles, CA

☆☆☆☆

Stephanie empowers her staff by letting them make decisions. She sets goals and puts them on their schedules. She gives gifts, and rewards her staff for special work well done.

"I always tell my staff just like it is. I have cried and layed it on the line for them. I let them know what we have to do to make things work. There is always an open door policy in my office. I want them to share back with me."

Stephanie Meyer of Stephan Cori; Fresno, CA

☆☆☆☆

"I feel fortunate to have the very best manager and buyer that a specialty store can have. With Ann Borrell's guidance and knowledge, we made the transition from a men's store to a men's and women's store almost overnight."

Jeff Maloy of Landon's; Ceres, CA

☆☆☆☆

"My excellent staff has been a miracle to me. They really help my business. I work a lot on a one to one with my staff. Communication is key to a great sales staff. I take my manager to market with me and let her make buying decisions. This gets her involved, and she feels as if she is even more a part of the store."

Mary Black of Hilda; Park City, UT

☆☆☆☆

"We train by accepting everyone's own style. Every one of my employees has their own unique style of selling, and I let them do it their way. I don't step on their toes.

"Money is the name of the game to motivate my staff, so I pay them well. I also give them a lot of freedom to create their own displays and merchandising, even if I don't really like what they have done."

Sue Gantz of My Sister's Circus; Chicago, IL

☆☆☆☆

"We support our teams from the corporate headquarters. We are always open to them and ask them to call us any time they need anything. Our biggest assets are the people who work for us. We must take good care of them."

Dick Oliver of Ames; Culver City, CA

☆☆☆☆

"This is a crazy business! There is such a small profit margin, and it is difficult to be successful because expenses are so high. The most ridiculous thing most retailers do is to put all their money in advertising, merchandising and store layout. They should be putting more money and time into their real bread and butter – their staff! They spend so little time and money training their salespeople. It's so nuts! If they would just put more into their staff, sales would take off.

"Some say, 'I have no time to work or to talk with my employees because I am so busy putting out fires.' If they worked with their staffs even five to 10 minutes per day, they would put out future fires before they ignited.

"Managers have a difficult job – they have to solve all the problems. They started out as salespeople and because they did such a good job, they moved up the ranks. Then they have to learn how to wear a different hat. They were good salespeople because they were self motivated. Then they are amazed when the rest of the world does not understand why they don't think as they do."

Wow, Bruce really touched a nerve with me. This really hit home. It makes so much sense, and it's simple to see that to create a great staff you must take the time, effort and money to do so. Your business is only going to be as good as your worst employee! Now, think about that! To create a positive image and environment in your business, you must have great employees!

Bruce Hird of Ames; Culver City, CA

☆☆☆☆

"Only about 10% of the staff we hire has previous retail training. I work with them on the floor, explaining merchandise, fabrics and how to coordinate it all. Then I show them how to sell. I want them to understand that when a customer is looking at something, that means they are showing an interest. It is the salesperson's job to approach and educate the customer about the product. That's when they can explain the benefits of buying."

Pat Kassul of Personality Shoppe; Rochelle, IL

☆☆☆☆

"I have great people working for me. We have fun, and we make it a happy environment in which to work. There is something to celebrate at every meeting. I don't get upset when something doesn't go right. Why waste your energy on negativity? We take problems and turn them into opportunities to enhance our business and make it better."

Delstar has a full time sales trainer and human resource manager. Much of the sales and management training is done at the home office. "We also track our customer service and merchandising of the stores by using in-store cameras.

"We teach small business skills to our staff and give them freedom with their ideas so they feel like business owners themselves."

Pam Del Duca of Delstar Group; Phoenix, AZ

☆☆☆☆

"The key to hiring a great staff is to always hire motivated people. I have monthly meetings during breakfast. This is the opportunity for everyone to get together and toss their ideas into the hat. I like input – I may be the leader, but I want everyone involved in every part of the business. I will inform the staff of what new merchandise is coming in so they know what they are going to have to sell ahead of time."

Carolyn Walker of Flair Boutique; Stockton, CA

☆☆☆☆

"Teamwork is key from day one!"

Manije Windell of Manije' Boutique; Burlingame, CA

☆☆☆☆

Mona is a great motivator. She is always working on goals and is prepared. "You must be prepared for each day. I prepare the night before each day. I know what I will have my staff work on. I set the pace for the day. I plan markdowns, re-merchandising ideas, receiving . . . you know busy work. It just never stops in this business.

"I give an add-on bonus to my salespeople of $1 per hour for their total number of hours in that month if they make the monthly quota. If they are over 10% from the previous year, I add a $50 bonus. The office manager lets them know where they are and how much more they need to sell to make that bonus. She is our store cheerleader."

Mona Cramer of Little House; LaPorte, IN

☆☆☆☆

"We have a great staff. We motivate them with a 10% commission and offer them all of their purchases at cost. Some of the staff came with a lot of experience, and they can make calls to customers better than I can."

Deanne Westen of Panache; San Jose, CA

☆☆☆☆

"I like to call my sales staff 'wardrobe coordinators,' because that is exactly who they are. They are so very creative.

"I pay my staff well, and they stay for years. Every Friday we have a one hour store meeting to discuss new stock that has come into the store. We have a very open meeting, and I always accept my employees' input. I listen to them and let them suggest what needs to be done in the store. It's important for me to listen to them because they spend the most time with the customers.

"My staff is so dedicated because I let them be open. They can do a better job at selling than I can. What the owner's job should be is to make sure everything works and then get to the bottom line of it all. If a customer is unhappy, I want to find out why and try to correct the problem as quickly as possible."

"I motivate myself to keep going by reading a lot. The only books I read are books that I can learn something from. I need to constantly be learning to keep ahead of my business. I need to be aware of what is going on around me too. I want to see what the customer is seeing and think how she thinks. I am passionate about what I do; it is such a big part of who I am."

Margo Miller of Margo's; Newhall, CA

☆☆☆☆

"I tell my staff to let the customers browse around and enjoy themselves. I want the customer to have a great time and to have my staff create new friends every day."

Susan Liss of Compliments; La Quinta, CA

☆☆☆☆

"I always set a level of business for the day. If our staff goes over that level, they get a bonus for that day. I add spiffs to sale items I want to sell. The spiffs range from $1 to $10. This gives the staff extra incentive to move the merchandise. When the staff works from one store to another, it motivates the other staff members. They want to compete to be the best store with the most volume."

Larry Langley of Casual Aire; Honolulu, HI

☆☆☆☆

"We are a non-commission store. We don't want the environment of too much competitiveness in our store. We work well as a team. We have weekly staff meetings to keep everyone informed. During those meetings, we are very open and

56

share our finances and business problems with our staff. It is important to let your staff know about your future goals."

Russ & Becky Casenhiser of La Galleria; Tustin, CA

☆☆☆☆

"I keep my staff motivated because we have a fun and open atmosphere in the store. I give my staff lots of perks and try not to put pressure on them."

Helen Lyall of Helen Lyall; Vallejo, CA

☆☆☆☆

"I have found that the most important thing I can do for my staff is to give them a lot of responsibility. I put them in charge of certain departments in the store. You must be very specific when you delegate if you want to get the job done your way. Put people to work in areas they are good at. If a certain department is having a problem, you know who to talk to about it."

Laura Garduno of Gee Lorretta; Albuquerque, NM

Chapter 5
STAYING AHEAD
OF THE COMPETITION

I am always – always – looking for new ways to take care of my customers. To give them better service and to be different from my competition.

Keeping a passion for business is key. I believe when you no longer have the passion, you won't work as hard on it, and you most definitely won't stay on top. You must also keep your staff up and motivated all the time. When I was going through a difficult personal time in my life, I saw it affect my staff and my business. As soon as I made a point to work on turning it around, my staff changed to a more positive atmosphere almost overnight. Your customers pick up on the attitude and atmosphere in your store. It's an unspoken language.

✫✫✫✫

"The key to staying ahead of my competition is my special contact with customers. I make a lot of personal calls and write personalized letters. I have a 'do anything to make it happen' attitude. I will even make house calls if the customer wants me to."

Marty Spencer of Chantilly Place; Riverside, CA

☆☆☆☆

"I always try to attend seminars at market. Seminars help me a lot! They can always make you look at something in a new light – it just puts it all in black and white for you."

Mary Black of Hilda; Park City, UT

☆☆☆☆

"In order to stay ahead of your competition, you have to know what your competition is doing and what is going on in your particular marketplace. We must strive to be better than the other cruise lines and to carry merchandise that is not found on every other ship.

"I must constantly see new vendors and know what is going on in other stores. Key items are essential to retail success these days.

"I am currently developing a QVC approach to marketing our gift shop merchandise via the televisions in the guest rooms."

Jennifer Chadney of Crystal Cruises; Los Angeles, CA

☆☆☆☆

Loree's favorite part of the business is when she is working on the floor with her customers. "This is my time to be creative – it really gets my creative juices flowing. I always schedule time for myself on the floor, even with my busy schedule. That time is for my customers and nothing else. I love to hear a customer comment how pleased she is with a purchase she made in my store years ago. When she says she is still wearing it and loving it, I know I've made a very satisfied customer. I always strive to carry quality merchandise that the customer can enjoy for a long time."

Loree is very involved in her community and local organizations. It is important to her to know her customers as her friends. "If I know my community and my customers, I can target their needs. By being honest and open, I have created many friends and loyal customers who will always come into my store for advice on an event they are planning to attend."

Loree Scarborough of G. Nonni; Long Beach, CA

☆☆☆☆

"The resort area is very difficult. I tried to trade down in the off season summer months, but it didn't work. I tried to purchase lower priced goods, and my customers did not what to buy them. Now, I buy the same all year and buy very few summer goods. I have found that my summer clients are not looking for summer items; they just want something new and different. About 90% of my business comes from tourists, so I have learned to cater to them all year long. We keep in constant touch with our out of town customers all year long.

"The only print advertising I do is in a local magazine to attract my tourists. I also use television advertising. For the money and the audience, it is the best buy in town during my high season months."

Georgia Rosenblat of Iris; Palm Springs, CA

☆☆☆☆

"We stick to what is easy for our customers. Displays make the sale. I know that when I go to a store, I always buy off the display. I don't want to take the time to look around. When our store is well merchandised, our customers will be more likely to buy."

Kent Hamrick of Eric Kent; Evanston, IL

☆☆☆☆

"We stay out in front of our competition because we enjoy this business and we do it with a passion. The day we don't enjoy our work is the time to move on. Attitude plays an important role in our success. You must be positive, directed and focused to keep your business running strong."

Pam Del Duca of Delstar Group; Phoenix, AZ

☆☆☆☆

"I will drop a line if other stores around me are carrying it. I don't carry lines that are in the department stores either. I think like a boutique all the time. I can't compete with the larger stores, so I don't try to."

Manije Windell of Manije' Boutique; Burlingame, CA

☆☆☆☆

"We are always checking out other stores when we travel to the mainland to see how lines are merchandised. This gives us fresh new ideas on display."

Larry Langley of Casual Aire; Honolulu, HI

☆☆☆☆

Chapter 6
PROMOTIONS
THAT CREATE SUCCESS

I love to have "theme" promotions. This is where I enjoy using my creative energy. I get an idea, and I expand on it to carry it all the way through my mailers, my store decor, my refreshments and more.

One of the most unique promotions I have had in my store was called "Shang-hi Surprise." I put discounts in fortune cookies and had the customer break one open for a discount or free gift. The store was decorated in an Oriental fashion, and I served Chinese food that was delivered to my store each day for lunch. My mailers were great. I folded my creative invitations in small Oriental cloth pouches and mailed them. The customers loved it and talked about this promotion for a long time.

I always try new promotions to keep my customers excited. I try to create retail entertainment. This gives the customer a reason to come into my store, and she feels as if she has been invited to a fun party.

Direct mail works well for me when I use my own mailing

list for these events. It is always the best response of any type of advertising I do. I also do a lot of local advertising to get new customers and tourists into my store. My advertising stands out from the norm. I set a tone and image for my business with these ads. Customers comment about our ads all the time, so they must be working. Most of my ads are just image ads to keep our name out there in front of the customer all the time.

☆☆☆☆

As I was on hold, waiting for Bill to answer my call, I was pleasantly entertained. Bill's store is advertised as you wait, and he even has his own store song, "When fantasy becomes reality." The advertisement tells the customer on hold about the store's location, credit card policies, store hours, layaway program, and special promotions. Unique ideas like this have helped make Bill a success.

"One of the best promotions is our Midnight Madness Sale. We start at 6:00 p.m. and offer a 20% discount. At 8:00 p.m. we offer a 30% discount. At 10:00 p.m. we offer a 40% discount. And from 12:00 a.m. to 1:00 a.m. our customers receive 50% off. Friday night is the best time for this sale. I have big spotlights in the parking lot to attract attention. I advertise on radio, call our best customers and send out a direct mail piece for our 11,000 customer mailing list. I will buy off-price goods at this time to keep my profit margins up. This promotion really gets our name out there. We plan this twice a year."

Bill Danches of Whatchamacallit; Dallas, TX

☆☆☆☆

"We mail seasonal fashion catalogs and preferred customer sale cards with an upscale look to add a good image to our

64

store. The catalog is printed through our New York buying office. We have to like about 80% of the catalog items they select to buy into the merchandise and order the catalogs.

"We get the best response from direct mail. One of the smartest things we have done is to keep building our mailing list and sending out direct mail often. It keeps our name in front of the customer all the time."

Pat Kassul of Personality Shoppe; Rochelle, IL

☆☆☆☆

"You can't do too many of the same events. You need to change them to make it interesting. Every store and location is different. You need to decide what works best for you."

Susan Warmbrodt of The Armoire; Coronado, CA

☆☆☆☆

"One of my best promotions is a Deer Hunter Widow Sale. On Fridays the men have gone hunting. It is a big deal in my area. We ask the wives to come in and shop with us from 7:00 p.m. to 10:00 p.m. for add-on discounts."

Example of the add-on discount program:

The customer receives 5% for coming into the store. She gets an additional 5% if she brings a friend. If she wears something she previously purchased, she gets another 5% discount. If she brings in a used bag from Evelyn's, she receives another 5% discount. If she wears a certain color, she can receive another 5% discount. If she brings in clothing to donate to a charity, she receives another 5% discount.

"The total savings cannot total more than a 30% discount. I change the program ideas every year to keep them new and interesting.

"When I do fashion shows for conventions, I charge a $200 fee. I then turn around and donate it back to the organization in the form of a gift certificate."

Kathleen Gubler of Evelyn's; St. George, UT

☆☆☆☆

"We do a lot of trunk shows – two or three a month. We plan to continually give the customer a reason to come back into the store. Since we have such a good relationship with our vendors, they are helpful with these shows and special orders. We keep in contact with our vendors all day long during our shows.

"We have created a marketing tool to track our customers by the lines of apparel they purchase. This micro marketing program captures the sales history of our customers and breaks down the list by vendor. This allows us to do a whole lot of extra things with our customer service."

Russ Casenhiser of La Gallery; Tustin, CA

☆☆☆☆

"Two-thirds of our customers are tourists, so I get involved in the mall activities and advertising. We often have in-mall fashion shows that bring the customers in."

Larry Shay of Private Collections: Las Vegas, NV

☆☆☆☆

"The problem with retail today is that everyone is competing for the same dollar. You can't sell them if you can't get them into your door. You constantly have to come up with new ways to get them to shop with you."

Kent Hamrick of Eric Kent; Evanston, IL

☆☆☆☆

"This year we had record months. Our best promotions have been created by using direct mail for trunk shows. Our mailers project a great image. They are tri-folds with a picture of the designer. Each salesperson must make 50 phone calls to tell our customers about the shows. You have to reach out and bring people into your stores now."

Dick Oliver of Ames; Culver City, CA

☆☆☆☆

"Four times a year we mail an 8 x 10 full color glossy postcard to all our customers. The photo postcard is a collage of our latest collection. We have a photographer take about 36 shots, and we select from the best. It then goes on the card with information about the new lines and styles. It is expensive, but it's worth it. We always get a good response."

Manije Windell of Manije' Boutique; Burlingame, CA

☆☆☆☆

"One of the best promotions I do is to have models on a regular basis at five local restaurants. All of my advertising indicates the show locations and times.

"I mail catalogs twice a year. I select 36 styles of only the best proven styles and lines for the catalog. My future goal is to get into the mail order business.

"The first week you don't have something going on, your business will be gone. I really believe in promoting and keeping my store's name out there."

Mona Cramer of Little House; LaPorte, IN

☆☆☆☆

"Fashion shows have been our best promotions this year. It is my lowest cost of advertising, and I get the best results. Every day from 12:00 to 2:00 p.m. we model at a local country club. This targets a lot of new customers from another area. I sell most of what I bring to the shows.

"Other promotions that work are our four day sale with 20% off everything in the store, and a physic day. We make appointments with a very well known physic for every 10 minutes. These promotions really bring in the customers. We have an ongoing two-for-one sale rack that really moves our older merchandise."

Deanne Westen of Panache; San Jose, CA

☆☆☆☆

"Whatever events you do in your store, do the best you can afford. This is a time when your customers need to feel that they are shopping in a store that cares about making them feel special. Do less if you have to – but do them up right."

Margo Miller of Margo's; Newhall, CA

☆☆☆☆

"The key to promotions is to track your best customers and work on getting them back into your store. We add excitement and fun to our mailers and promotional events.

"During the holidays we mail out golden walnuts to our best customers. They will bring in the nut for us to crack open. Inside is a different color bead which indicates the dollar discount amount."

Laura Garduno of Gee Lorretta; Albuquerque, NM

Chapter 7
TO MARKET . . .TO MARKET
HOW THE STARS DO THEIR BUYING

Always plan out your markets before you go. Time is money when you are at market. The more you see, the better your buying will be. The more organized you are at market, the more you will accomplish. It is such an important part of our job. Good buying skills are one of the greatest assets any retail store owner can have. These skills can make or break your business.

I go to market with a complete vendor list organized by floor and category. I have a detailed list for every market I attend across the country. I can't leave home without it. The list includes showroom numbers, salesperson's name and type of line. This list is compiled and set up on my computer. I run a copy of the market list before I leave for market and highlight the lines I need to see for that season. After I return from market, I update my list. Since lines move around all the time, it's important to keep a good track record of who is carrying what line.

When I hear about a new line or see it in another store or catalog, I will make a note of it and toss it into my market file. I will research the line before I go to market by calling the salesperson and inquiring about the price points and also where the line is carried at other stores in my area. This saves me the extra time I need at market.

I do not leave paper at market unless it is a quick delivery or a reorder. I break down the delivery dates into groups and work with one month at a time. I will then compare lines, price points, quality and previous sales records if available. I write orders on my store order forms and fax them to my sales associates within a few days. I try not to wait on sending my orders in because waiting too long affects my buying. It is important to have a mental picture when selecting color, sizes and styles. And if I can't remember the line after a few days, I don't need it anyway. I make working on those orders the day after I return from market a priority. This way I am still in my market mind-set before I return to the store and get back into the day to day end of my business again.

I have an excellent rapport with my sales associates. They are an important part of my business. This helps me out with special orders and trunk shows, and builds a good helpful friendship and shared networking source. I give my sales associates referrals all the time — it comes back to me many times over. My ex-husband was a clothing sales representative for 20 years, so I have learned what it is like on both sides of the business. This has helped me to understand and support my sales associates throughout the years. They have a hard job to do, and they can do it better with good communication and respect from their buyers.

I make very few appointments at market because I always want to leave time open to find new lines. I call back only those few showrooms that are very busy at market to set up a time so that I can work quickly. If a line is "hot," I will make an appointment to let my salesperson know I am interested and that I will definitely be in to view the collection. I don't want my competition getting the line before I do if it is something I know can work for me.

"I try to attend every show that I can. I won't buy anything, no matter how good, if it is sold at stores around me. I do a lot of my buying at the New York shows to stay different from my competition on the West Coast. I try to get together with other specialty store owners from other states for their input."

Georgia Rosenblat of Iris; Palm Springs, CA

☆☆☆☆

Sylvia has been buying in New York for 50 years. She has been told that she is the toughest buyer there is. Sylvia takes that as a wonderful compliment. If shopping the market extensively, comparing lines and looking for the best price is considered tough, then we can all learn to get a little tougher.

"New York has changed over the years. Manufacturers are cutting closer to deliveries. Therefore, there is not as much off-price as there used to be. Everyone is thinking big stores — they don't want to ship to a lot of different stores. They would rather ship to one big store. That is why the big guys are getting most of the off-price now.

"I get frustrated with delivery dates. When they change a date on me, it affects my business. If I ordered coats for September delivery, I don't want them in October or November when my customers have already purchased a coat from another store."

Sylvia never stops looking for new and innovative lines in the market. She recently joined a large buying office in New York, looking for a new direction. No one can ever think they know it all or that they can find it all out there by themselves.

Good buyers know this, and will network or join forces with an office to help them with this "treasure hunt" for the best selections.

Sylvia Rosett of Caplan's, Chicago, IL

☆☆☆☆

Loree travels to many markets outside of her area to stay unique and different from the competition. She purchases from the coast of Italy and has special showings in her store. She has even created her own merchandise by selecting from Italian fabrics. Loree also attends the Style Works and Premiere Apparel shows in New York and always finds new lines. "Some of these lines are great California resources that I may not have found while I was attending the Los Angeles Market."

Even though she keeps her merchandise mix somewhat the same, Loree has learned to be a great buyer from listening to what her customers' wants and needs are.

Loree Scarborough of G. Nonni; Long Beach, CA

☆☆☆☆

"I work with a buying office in Los Angeles to find hot items and for outside consulting. I believe that you must have someone in the market all the time so that you know what is going on at all times. This business changes so fast. It takes a team of three to buy for my store: myself, my manager and my buying office."

Larry Shay of Private Collections; Las Vegas, NV

☆☆☆☆

"I shop all the major markets. I can't afford to miss a new trend, especially in the young men's department. I spend five days at the Magic Show (men's Las Vegas market). My manager and I run ourselves ragged at the shows before we are finished. We want to see everything and find all the hot lines. We need to move quickly on those lines to get in and out of them at the right time. The biggest challenge is to have the top lines in a timely manner. Brand names are important in the young men's business, but not in the contemporary women's lines.

"While at market, I meet with my networking group. It consists of about 13 stores. We all stay at the same hotel and meet each morning before the show at a special room reserved for us at that hotel. I learn so much from this group. We all have our own ideas and lines to share. Sometimes we will buy together to get a better price on a large quantity.

"I also attend seminars at market to get new ideas. I sometimes hear what I already know, but have forgotten the importance of putting that knowledge into action."

Jeff Maloy of Landon's; Ceres, CA

☆☆☆☆

"I learned to be a good buyer the hard way – the school of hard knocks was my best education. I learned to accept markdowns, and I will mark down my buying mistakes quickly. If it is a loser and not working out – get rid of it fast! Make room for new, fresh merchandise."

Susan Warmbrodt of The Armoire; Coronado, CA

☆☆☆☆

Pat has been shopping the market in New York for so many years that she knows how to get the best prices. Because she has excellent credit in her business, she can work better deals. "I know how to tactfully ask for a discount on a line. I explain to them that I have a small store, but if it sells I will reorder fast.

"I'll tell my sales associates that the line looks great, but that I could do better if I received a discount. I try to show them that it is a win-win situation. The off-price lines have to look as good as the regular priced lines to be a good buy. You need the extra margin on some lines to stay ahead in business. New York deals because so many stores are closing and these companies are cutting closer to the delivery dates.

"I buy only four to six pieces of an item. You don't have to buy too much of any one item. If my sales associates ask for more, I say go ahead and put my order through as written. If they ship it, good. If not, I figure I don't need it. I will receive about 90% of what I order with the quantities I want this way.

"I buy holiday lines in November when I can get them for 40% off. Holiday is a difficult season because you take too many markdowns. In January, I buy some spring at a discounted price. I always plan to leave some of my open-to-buy money open for quick deliveries on off-price.

"I change the shipping dates to work for us, not just what the salesperson states the delivery is. It is our money and our store. I know when I need the merchandise and when it will sell. There is a lot of merchandise out there, so I can always find something else, unless it is to die for, of course.

"We have an open-to-buy budget with a breakdown into four quarters. Off-price accounts for 30 to 40% of our stock year round. We follow our budget closely, thus controlling our inventory and always being open for good off-price merchandise."

Pat Kassul of Personality Shoppe, Rochelle, IL

☆☆☆☆

"When I started out as a buyer, I told my salespeople to be gentle to me – I'm new at this. I now know my likes and dislikes. I keep a mental picture of my customer in mind. The most important thing to do is to keep your image – I'm obsessed with image!"

Dick Oliver of Ames; Culver City, CA

☆☆☆☆

"We strategically plan our buying by categories of merchandise in the store. Then we break it down further with detailed information. It is difficult to get a handle on this at first, but after you have a few years of data, it works easily."

Russ & Becky Casenhiser of La Galleria; Tustin, CA

☆☆☆☆

What makes Kent a great buyer is that he has a good eye for the latest trends. He gets in and out of the latest items before his competition does. I was really blown away when Kent told me that he has never worked with an open-to-buy in his many years of retail. Do not try this trick in your own store! The magic that Kent has is from his many years of experience and his own innate sense.

"If I don't like it, I don't buy it, and I think that my customers like what I like. Why should I buy something just because I have money to spend — I'm just buying a markdown! It is more difficult buying now. There is no newness, nothing is jumping out there telling me to buy, and if I feel that way, my customer will also."

Kent Hamrick of Eric Kent; Evanston, IL

☆☆☆☆

"Don't fill your stores up with too much of the same look. Make it look like a specialty store by having a lot of unique looks. Make a nice story of lots of groups.

"I buy very close to delivery dates. You can commit yourself better when you know what is going on in your store."

Laura Garduno of Gee Lorretta; Albuquerque, NM

☆☆☆☆

"I'm gutsy when trying new lines — I don't play it safe. If you want to be unique, you just have to go ahead and go for it, whether you think it is safe or not."

Helen Lyall of Helen Lyall; Vallejo, CA

☆☆☆☆

"I am very discriminating in my buying. I always want merchandise that is different, interesting and unusual. I find new lines in magazines, or I will see someone wearing something great and ask her about it. I will buy new lines myself at retail to check them out and see how I like them. It costs less than buying an entire rack of markdowns."

Susan Liss of Compliments; La Quinta, CA

"I can make buying decisions quickly. I'm a seamstress, so I understand the construction of the garment. When I like something, I don't have to think about it. I will write the order right then and leave paper. I go totally by my instincts since I have done it for so long. I can tell what my open-to-buy is without even having to total up my orders. The worst buy I could ever make is when the item has a bad fit, because if it fits – I will sell it.

"I have a good rapport with my sales associates. I think of them as a close family. I will always acknowledge what they do for me, respect their time and be polite."

Margo Miller of Margo's; Newhall, CA

☆☆☆☆

"I try to really zero in on key lines, lines that get strong recognition. I will carry these lines extensively, keeping stocked with them all the time. At first I didn't make money at this, but I kept building on it and now it is very profitable.

"I always take 20% off my open-to-buy to try new lines and items. I won't buy it if I don't have a customer in mind who I think will love it. I will always need to try something different and out of the ordinary to keep my customers interested."

Mona Cramer of Little House; LaPorte, IN

☆☆☆☆

"I know what I want when I see it. I make fast decisions on my buying. You're going to second guess no matter what, so you need to learn to work fast and move on. I dislike seeing other buyers sitting there and suffering over their decisions to buy. You need to know your store's strength in sizes and looks, and if you can sell upper end or not. Don't back down from your store's focus. Don't ever lose your direction or back down from your unique item type of lines. Stay focused continually. It is not the 80's any more — it is not easy. But you don't have to change your store for the looks you love. If you love it — your customers will too."

Carolyn Walker of Flair Boutique; Stockton, CA

☆☆☆☆

"When I go to market, I just look around the first day. I check on everything out there, then I go back and review the lines and place orders. I will leave paper if I know a line is good or that I can sell it. I know my customers' tastes and what colors work best. Most of the time I can tell what will sell. I'm not always on, but no one can be right all the time — that's retail."

Manije Windell of Manije' Boutique; Burlingame, CA

☆☆☆☆

Larry and his sister Jody run three stores. They attend markets together to buy for the stores. When they return, they work together as a team. Larry is the marketing manager who decides how many of a style they will buy — he's the numbers man. Jody has a flair for what is hot and what is not. As a team, they make fewer buying errors.

"We can reorder our best styles often because we have a new customer base every five to seven days. Sometimes we reorder as many as three to five times.

"I always listen to what other buyers are saying at the markets. When I am in an elevator and a buyer is talking about a certain line that is doing well, I'll go check it out right away."

Larry Langley of Casual Aire; Honolulu, HI

"I constantly see new vendors, especially new designers who are just starting out. They are often creative and end up being very loyal to me. I am constantly in the market and the retail stores as well to determine hot items and fashion changes."

Jennifer Chadney of Crystal Cruises; Los Angeles, CA

Mary has learned to have the right merchandise at the right time. She knows what is selling and reorders fast, moving merchandise quickly. She buys what she likes. That way her store takes on her personality. "I feel it is important to buy what I like because I could not sell it if I didn't like it. You can't get caught up in what some salespeople say when they don't even know your store. If you don't think it's for you, stick to your guns."

Mary Black of Hilda; Park City, Utah

☆☆☆☆

"I spend a lot of time and money traveling to markets to see what is happening. I am always looking for different, artsy and creative merchandise. This business is personal to me, I buy what I like. Luckily, I have learned to have a good eye for fashion with my many years of experience. I try to stay away from very high end goods, and that is difficult at times when you carry the unique type of inventory that I do. But if it is too high end, I get outside of my niche market."

Sue Gantz of My Sister's Circus; Chicago, IL

☆☆☆☆

"I really do my homework before I go to market. I know what has sold and what people are asking for. I get reports from all my top salespeople and compare their comments with my sales reports. My sales reports are very complete, including sales, layaways, discounts and markdowns.

"I have meetings with my staff before markets. I like to know everything that goes on sale and why. I don't want to make the same mistake again. You must be aware of the styles and the reason something had to be marked down."

Audrey Fu of Villa Roma & Chocolates for Breakfast; Honolulu, HI

Chapter 8
WHAT THE STARS ARE SAYING ABOUT THE FUTURE

This business is much more difficult now with added competition and discount stores. But I feel that you can not only survive, but also thrive if you always set very high goals for yourself and keep on learning and changing with your business. You cannot get stale – you must always stay fresh and new. Move your store's inventory around all the time; keep it interesting and fun. Don't lose interest in your business. If you stop working on it, it will show in less than six months and really affect your volume. I know this because it has happened to me – you must stay interested and focused all the time.

My business is in a resort community where tourism is our #1 industry. People love to shop the wonderful specialty stores in this area because we have different merchandise from what can be found in their home towns. The difficult part of owning a store in a tourist area is the ever-increasing rent expenditures. But we will always have an active audience. Specialty stores will always be important in a tourist area as part of entertainment shopping.

☆☆☆☆

"There will always be emotion in our business, and people will always want that special customer service and attention that they get from the specialty stores.

"The number one thing that attracts a customer is color. After that it is style. The customer will always have the need to see the merchandise firsthand and to feel the emotion of the purchase."

Kent Hamrick of Eric Kent; Evanston, IL

☆☆☆☆

"There will be more consolidation of retailers. It will not be unusual to see one large corporation owning 20 to 30 stores in one mall. The smaller retailer will be like the Jurassic Park of retailing within the next 10 years.

"I don't want to see this industry of smaller retailers die. But it is getting harder to overcome expenses. Margins have not gone up, yet overhead has. We will have to convince the manufacturers to give us more to help us out in the form of better terms and discounts."

Dick Oliver of Ames; Culver City, CA

☆☆☆☆

"Business is a lot harder now than in the 60's when you could sell just about anything to anyone. You need to work harder and smarter now. What I have enjoyed about this business for so many years is that retail is ever-changing – every day is different and new!"

Loree Scarborough of G. Nonni; Long Beach, CA

☆☆☆☆

"There will always be a need for specialty shops. But my fear is that there will also be too many discount stores. I can see that people don't feel the same and care as much as they used to about their dress. In terms of dressing lifestyle, people are becoming very casual. There are no real fashion heroes out there now. There's not enough newness in the market-

place. It's either too casual or too dated. Designers need to work on building excitement again."

Marty Spencer of Chantilly Place; Riverside, CA

☆☆☆☆

"Customers will always come back to the stores that give them great service and go out of their way to do nice things for them. If you find your special niche, they will want it and will pay for it. That is what keeps it going for us."

Sue Gantz of My Sister's Circus; Chicago, IL

☆☆☆☆

"This industry scares me today. It has lost its flair, and the only stores that will survive are the ones that have kept their flair. No one is taking big risks in our industry today. Fashion and design are, therefore, not as exciting as they could be."

Kenneth Mizel of Rodier.Paris; Ramsey, NJ

☆☆☆☆

"I see more mail order and computer retailing for the future. We have less time now, so it is hard to find free time to go shopping.

"The department stores currently have so much of the same merchandise. This has to change in order to regain some of the old loyalty that department stores used to have."

Jennifer Chadney of Crystal Cruises; Los Angeles, CA

☆☆☆☆

"Customers will be more price conscious and will want more

value for their money. They will not be concerned with labels and designer names as much as quality. As more designer lines are sold to discounters, they won't be as important to the customer."

Larry Shay of Private Collections; Las Vegas, NV

☆☆☆☆

"The mega discount malls will faze out many smaller stores. The discount stores are getting smarter. The merchandise is displayed nicely, and some of these stories even look like specialty shops. They do not offer as big of discounts as consumers believe they do, but the merchandise is more current than it has been in the past."

Pat Kassul of Personality Shoppe; Rochelle, IL

☆☆☆☆

"I plan to stay in business as long as I can. I am concerned about the future of the small specialty stores though. People are so busy now. Shopping is being made easier for them with QVC, catalogs and factory outlets."

Susan Warmbrodt of The Armoire; Coronado, CA

☆☆☆☆

"If you don't have what the department stores are carrying, you will always bring customers back because you are special and different."

Carolyn Walker of Flair Boutique; Stockton, CA

☆☆☆☆

"We will need more service than ever before. I believe that women will start to buy like men, two big buys a year. Customers will expect the extra service and attention. Women want exclusivity as much as possible. When a line is seen by the customer in major catalogs and in too many major retail chains, it loses its fashion appeal."

Margo Miller of Margo's; Newhall, CA

☆☆☆☆

"It will be a tough go in the future of retailing. I see the big stores having too many sales. The outlet malls are cutting into some of our sales profits. I will sometimes give my customers a discount to compete with a line they can buy at the outlet stores near me. You will have to really take care of your customers to keep them out of the outlets and coming to you because of your service."

Helen Lyall of Helen Lyall; Vallejo, CA

☆☆☆☆

"I believe that the smaller stores will do even more business because this is where the customer can come to get good service. Customers will get tired of shopping the big stores and going through the racks and racks of items to find what they want."

Laura Garduno of Gee Lorretta; Albuquerque, NM

☆☆☆☆

"Smaller stores will survive if they stay unique. There are unknown designers out there who are begging to be recognized.

"You must have great service! If a customer wants a special

order that costs only $19 – order it for them. It is a lot of hard work, but the customer will appreciate that service and come back for more.

Audrey Fu of Villa Roma & Chocolates for Breakfast; Honolulu, HI

☆☆☆☆

"Specialty stores will not change very much within the next five years. I don't see a big growth or decline in the number of stores. But eventually customer service will be the only thing that the smaller specialty stores will have to compete over the large stores."

Russ Casenhiser of La Galleria; Tustin, CA

☆☆☆☆

"We change lives in this business every day. It is such an emotional business. Our stores are connected to the human condition. We will not fold if the economy is falling apart because there will always be the needs we fill with emotion. When people buy, they buy for an emotional fix. People will always be falling in love and out of love. That's when they want something to make them feel better."

"Feel the dreams you create, and you will have an incredible future!"

Bruce Hird of Ames; Culver City, CA

Chapter 9
ADVICE FROM THE STARS

The best business advice I ever received was from my father. He would always tell me, "Do it now!" He even bought a sign for my desk with this saying on it that I looked at every day. That made me a doer – not just talking about plans and goals – accomplishing them.

Always have goals and plans in place for your business. Revise this plan constantly. Keep doing what works and make changes where you need to, no matter how drastic they may be.

Find a business mentor. You should always pay attention to other successful people and learn from them. You can never stop learning. If you do, you stop growing. Hire consultants to help you with new marketing ideas and to learn good business skills. I hire consultants for new ideas. They will work with you by sharing those ideas and new insights into your business. You don't have to sign a contract with many consultants. Just bring them in when you need some new knowledge or support. Fees can range from $75 to $100 per hour. Most of the consultants I have found are other successful business people that I meet at seminars and networking functions. Just ask if you could hire them to do some brainstorming for an hour to see how they work out for you. Never assume that you can just ask people to lunch and pick their brain for free. A good business person understands that the consultant's time is valuable also and should expect to pay for that time.

Stay on top of things in your business, such as your paperwork and your credit. Once you start digging yourself a hole by getting behind on your bills, it is very difficult to get back on track in this business. When credit gets bad, good lines won't ship, and this in turn affects sales. I have seen this happen to other stores too often. If you get in a bind with your bills, make some major adjustments to get back on track. Call up your manufacturers and communicate to them what is going on. Cancel orders and cut back on your expenses if you must to hang in there.

Don't give up – some people give up too soon. Keep fighting to make it work. Many give up just before they were becoming successful. Many businesses that close their doors are even showing a profit on their books.

☆☆☆☆

"Listen to your sales associates. You can learn a lot from them, and they can be a big help to your business.

"Check postage on your shipments. Weigh the package when it comes in. If the fee is too high, I send out a form along with my payment stating the deduction. I have never had a company question the deduction. Some companies will even charge for special handling, so I will charge them back for my time too. It's fair trade.

"Check dates on your packaging slip when an order comes

in. Some companies will date the invoice 10 days to two weeks before it was shipped.

"Learn how to grow your business by attending seminars and reading books."

Kathleen Gubler of Evelyn's; St. George, UT

☆☆☆☆

"Many stores went under in the 90's because the owners were not there. You have to be there and be on the floor. You must become involved to stay in business now."

Barbara Strassberger of Prestige; Palo Alto, CA

☆☆☆☆

"Keep your overhead as small as possible. Don't get carried away with your ego. If you are a small specialty store – stay out of the malls. You can sell as much out of 800 square feet as you can out of 1,600 square feet. Keep a smaller store full, and it will look better. When you think of expanding and you are doing a nice business, remember the old saying – if it ain't broken, don't fix it! Keep it simple – keep it small!"

Georgia Rosenblat of Iris; Palm Springs, CA

☆☆☆☆

"Truly, if I was to tell someone to go into business today, I would suggest that they already have some type of following. Have a following from a country club or some other organization to bring people into your store from the very beginning.

"It is hard to pay the rents and cover the expenses without

going in with a lot of capital. When you start out, you should have one-quarter million minimum to get established. You will need to buy inventory, do your build out and establish credit. Don't go in under-capitalized because it is just too difficult to have staying power and compete."

Sylvia Rosett of Caplan's; Chicago, IL

☆☆☆☆

"You have to keep doing a little something all the time. It puts your name out there to your community. Use any excuse for a party or event in your store to keep the excitement happening."

Loree Scarborough of G. Nonni; Long Beach, CA

☆☆☆☆

"If you want to expand your business, really ask yourself, 'why???' What studies have you done? Are you competing against yourself or with another store that is too close? Research the market and get all the facts first."

Audrey Fu of Villa Roma & Chocolates for Breakfast; Honolulu, HI

☆☆☆☆

"Get training from a department store, or better yet, a specialty store chain. Work on the sales floor and learn the business. A specialty store can still take chances and risks. You can learn a lot and have fun learning from a company that is growing."

Kenneth Mizel of Rodier.Paris; Ramsey, NJ

☆☆☆☆

"Don't talk too much – learn to listen to your customers. This was the best advice I received from one of my first bosses.

"Don't ever think you know it all – EVER!"

Stephanie Meyer of Stephan Cori; Fresno, CA

☆☆☆☆

"Be careful! Know what you are doing before you leap, because this is a difficult business."

Sue Gantz of My Sister's Circus; Chicago, IL

☆☆☆☆

"Never neglect your current customers. They contribute to 80% of your sales. It takes you twice as long to acquire a new customer as it does to keep a current customer.

"Gain as much knowledge as you can from your markets and networking with other retailers. Continue growing by adding new ideas to your business.

"There is a need to add off-price merchandise to your mix. Find out how to get off-price from your manufacturers."

Pat Kassul of Personality Shoppe; Rochelle, IL

☆☆☆☆

"Research your market. See what your competition is doing before you open a store. Plan plenty of money for mistakes, and plan not to make a profit for at least one year. Learn what off-price means.

"Don't get disappointed — Keep on trying."

Bill Danches of Whatchamacallit; Dallas, TX

☆☆☆☆

"Don't go into a mall location. The rent is too high, and the clientele is difficult for a specialty store. The malls have a younger customer, too many problems, and too long of hours. The best thing I ever did for my business was to move out of the mall."

Laura Garduno of Gee Lorretta; Albuquerque, NM

☆☆☆☆

"Control your inventory!!! Money is getting tight, and factors are not as lenient as they used to be. If you buy too much at first, you can get into financial problems fast. You must have good credit in this business. It is very important to making it a success. Start out by being careful with your open to buy.

"It's not enough to love clothes and people to open up a store. You have to really work on building your business. Start working on it, and keep up your pace. Expect to build your business by keeping up with that pace.

"Know what image you want to project and what type of customer you want to attract. Stick with that image all the time. You cannot be everything to everyone. One of the biggest mistakes retailers make is that they buy all over the board. In a small operation you can't do it all. Always ask yourself, 'What do I want to be and what image do I want to project?'"

Helen Lyall of Helen Lyall; Vallejo, CA

☆☆☆☆

"Be more conservative in the quantity you buy at times and find better quality items. Really look for items — this balances out the lemons you buy."

Susan Liss of Compliments; La Quinta, CA

☆☆☆☆

"My biggest lesson is this business was not to over buy.

"You need to know how to display properly to make it look interesting and pulled together. Take that extra time and effort to merchandise right — to have the store always looking fresh and comfortable."

Deanne Westen of Panache; San Jose, CA

☆☆☆☆

"Never lose your vision. If you do, it's over! Stores perish for the lack of vision. Always set short and long term goals.

"If a customer wants a discount, I won't move off my borders. It is not fair to other customers. Having unequal weight in my pockets will throw me off. If the word gets around, it could ruin your business reputation. Keep your standards, and don't lower prices unless you want to be a discounter."

Mona Cramer of Little House; LaPorte, IN

☆☆☆☆

"Don't worry about what everyone else is doing. Focus on what you want to do. Be decisive, and stick with your decisions. Be confident! Know your customer base and area when you put that package together for your business. Let your package be your package – no one else's.

"I love to go to work every day. I am as happy at work as I am at home. I keep it exciting all the time. You can stay up and positive if you don't have negative people around you."

Carolyn Walker of Flair Boutique; Stockton, CA

☆☆☆☆

"Find people who know business well and hire them. Hire a good store manager who has experience from another quality store. This will save you from making tons of mistakes along the way.

"You may select a great location for your store, in a busy shopping center, but it is so important to select a good location within that center. Every shopping center has areas that have better visibility and traffic flow than others. Ask yourself where you can be seen by the most people."

Russ Casenhiser of La Galleria; Tustin, CA

☆☆☆☆

"Believe in yourself and what you are doing! Don't be willing to throw in the towel when the going gets tough. Plan well. There is a lot of competition out there. Get market studies, and have some type of strategic planning in the works.

"Sit by the location you are considering and watch the traffic. Check the phone book for other similar businesses, and know who your competition is and where it is located.

"Get business training at a local community college or business center.

"Find mentors to help you with ideas. When you become successful, you can turn around and help someone else.

"Be kind to yourself, and get lots of exercise. It will keep you motivated and give you the energy you need to keep on going. Learn to have fun, and laugh at yourself. Don't be too serious all the time.

"There is no one right way to do something, so don't be afraid to do it your way."

Pam Del Duca of Delstar Group; Phoenix, AZ

☆☆☆☆

"Displaying your merchandise is the most important thing in this industry. Use your slow moving items to re-merchandise your store. Pieces that are left from a group may work well with something else in your store. Learn to be creative and have a good eye to keep your merchandise away from the markdown rack."

Manije Windell of Manije' Boutique; Burlingame, CA

☆☆☆☆

"Don't be afraid to miss dinner and keep on working, even if you have to work 60 to 70 hours a week sometimes. Work when it's needed to make it happen. You have to put a lot of time in to make it work well. If you can't get up with a happy face on every day because you are not enjoying your work, get another job. If you don't like it, don't do it! Life is just too short for that."

Larry Shay of Casual Aire; Honolulu, HI

☆☆☆☆

Top 10 Tips from a star retailer:

1. Research and know your customers.

2. Think "key" items.

3. Train your staff on a daily basis.

4. Keep focused.

5. Maintain a good customer service profile at all times.

6. Purchase quality merchandise that you are proud of.

7. Be creative and different.

8. Maintain high visual presentation standards at all times.

9. Get feedback from successful people in business.

10. Take the emotion out of buying decisions, and base them on actual sales performance.

Jennifer Chadney of Crystal Cruises; Los Angeles, CA

☆☆☆☆

Order Blank

I would like additional copies of *TRADE SECRETS OF RETAIL STARS*.

Quantity ordered _____ .

Cost $19.95 Plus $2.00 shipping and handling per book.

Make money on resale of this book or give as gifts to your business associates. Volume purchases are available at discounted prices. Call for pricing.

☐ I am interested in learning more about Debbie Allen's seminars. Please send me a complete portfolio, seminar information and free demo video.

☐ Please add me to your mailing list to receive information about new products and seminar locations.

Send to:

IMAGE DYNAMICS, INC.

7001 N. Scottsdale Road, Suite #120 • Scottsdale, AZ 85253

Phone (602) 948-7753 • Fax (602) 948-7487 • Voice mail 800-559-3142

Complete the information below, and mail or fax today. We accept the following credit cards: Visa, MasterCharge, Discover/Novus, or American Express.

Name_____

Address_____

City _____ State _____ Zip_____

Phone (   )_____ Fax (   )_____

Credit Card #_____ Exp. Date _____

Signature X _____ Date _____

Success Showcase Publication

ABOUT THE AUTHOR

Debbie Allen has been a business owner for 20 years. During the past 12 years, she has owned and operated three retail stores, specializing in contemporary women's apparel, accessories and gifts. Allen's current store, is located in Scottsdale, Arizona.

Allen is listed in Who's Who of Arizona Woman in Business and Scottsdale's Most Achieving Women. She has been nominated for such prestigious awards as Entrepreneur of The Year, the Athena Award, and Arizona Business Woman of the Year. Allen is a board member of the National Speakers Association Arizona Chapter.

Allen's vast business experience and incredible mentors have given her the rich knowledge she now has to share with audiences across the nation. Her dynamic presentations always gain her rave reviews.

Allen's client base includes major apparel and gift markets, business conventions, chambers of commerce and merchants' associations nationally.

Debbie Allen can share her enthusiasm and passion for business with your organization. For information on Allen's latest seminars, contact her directly through Image Dynamics, Inc., 7001 N. Scottsdale Road, Suite #120, Scottsdale, AZ 85253. Call: office, (602) 948-7753; or voice mail, 800 559-3142. Fax: (602) 948-7753.